METRE READINGS

Poems by Philip Brown

Illustrations by Philip Moss

Cover design by June Cook

Cover photograph by Transco

With all best wishes
phil

All proceeds from the sale of
this book will go to charity.

First published in 2002 by Philip Brown,
12, Court Gardens, Hempsted, Gloucester GL2 5JX.

All proceeds from the sale of this book will be donated
to charity.

Text   © Philip Brown 2002

Illustrations   © Philip Moss 2002

Cover design   © June Cook 2002

Cover photograph © Transco 2002

ISBN 0 9541380 0 7

Text set in Times New Roman.
Cover text set in Goudy Old Style.

Printed in Midsomer Norton by Bookcraft Ltd.

CONTENTS

ILLUSTRATIONS

ACKNOWLEDGEMENTS

I am very grateful to Philip Moss for providing the illustrations, and to June Cook for designing the cover. I would also like to thank Transco for supplying the cover photograph, and for their donation to charity as a gesture of support for this project.

Poems in this collection have appeared in the following publications: "Candelabrum", "The Citizen", "C.P.R. International", "Diss Writers Open Anthology (2000)", "Focus" (British Science Fiction Association), Gloucester Civic Trust 10th. Annual Report, "Hare's Breadth", "iota", "The Lakes Leader", "News and Views" (The Anglo-Danish Society), "Out in the Open" (Chiltern Writers), "Poetic Hours", "Poetry Now", "Poetry Life", "South West Review", "20 Years of 20th. Century Poetry (Staple)", "Sunflower Dawn" (St. Michael's Hospice, Hereford), Three Choirs Festival Programme (1986), "Weyfarers" and "Write to the Edge Again".

Edward Elgar: (1857-1934)
I have adapted the following sources:
A.J.J. - letters from A.J. Jaeger to Dora Penny; **D.P.** - "Memories of a Variation" by Dora Penny, with thanks for permission to Claud Powell and the Scolar Press; **H.J.W.** - "My life of Music" by Sir Henry Wood, with thanks to Victor Gollancz Ltd. for permission; **G.B.S.** - letter and postcard from Shaw to the composer, with thanks for permission to the Society of Authors; **H.R.** - letter from the composer to Hans Richter, with thanks for permission to R.W. Montgomery and the Elgar Will Trust; **T.E.L.** - letter from Lawrence to the composer, with thanks for permission to the Trustees of the Seven Pillars of Wisdom Trust.

Erratum
Page 7, line 20
Should read blinding

The central character in "Conjurer, Actor, Trickster ... " is not intended to portray any real person, living or dead. The views he expresses are not to be attributed to any charity on whose behalf this book is sold.

*

"At the Literary Festival" portrays a memorable afternoon in unfavourable circumstances.   Since then, the Cheltenham Festival Bookshop has been moved to the marquee, while most poetry readings take place in the Pillar Room.

*

meter: an apparatus for measuring

metre (1): the regulated succession of groups of syllables (long and short, stressed and unstressed) in which poetry is ... written

The Chambers Dictionary

ANTIPHONAL

Time is the bond that is our binding
Time is the warp that is our weaving
Time is the brand that is our burning
Time is the grave that is our grieving
Time is the blaze that is our blinding
Time is the life that is our leaving

Love is the gaze that is our guarding
Love is the shock that is our shaking
Love is the kiss that is our keeping
Love is the bread that is our breaking
Love is the sigh that is our sleeping
Love is the warmth that is our waking

Time is the sea that is our sharing
Time is the frost that is our fearing
Time is the wind that is our warning
Time is the sun that is our searing
Time is the moon that is our mourning
Time is the storm that is our steering

Love is the maze that is our meeting
Love is the blaze that is our binding
Love is the gift that is our glancing
Love is the weft that is our winding
Love is the day that is our dancing
Love is the bond that is our binding

THE BALLAD OF TIME AND LOVE

It seemed to be an ancient time,
    A distant distant land,
A cemetery beside the sea
    Invaded by the sand.

The scenes that passed across his mind
    Like drifting drifting smoke
Were like a dream that troubled him
    The moment he awoke.

The summer ball where time stood still
    And held them held them fast:
The separation which began
    Their journey to the past:

The limping man who looked at them
    With kindly kindly gaze
And faded as they wandered in
    The fast-receding maze.

The stately dance, the Tudor masque,
    The cunning cunning trial:
The barons' vote administered
    With mediaeval guile.

"This young man's crime, to fall in love
    With open open eyes."
"Guilty" - "Guilty" - "Innocent":
    Release, but in disguise.

"The vote is split, so you must watch
    The trial the trial to come,
But may not make a single move:
    Observe: be still: be dumb."

It was the girl: he called her name:
    "A foolish foolish crime:
You'll lose her now, and travel till
    You pierce the mists of time."

He twisted in a dizzy world
    Of blinding blinding light,
Of tumbling planets, spinning stars,
    And voices in the night,

Until he stopped and saw at last
    A flowing flowing tide
That lapped against the tilting tombs
    Of lovers who had died.

"I saw the trials: there was no crime":
    The voice the voice was clear:
He turned to see, not one, but two:
    "Not lost, for she is here."

"Stand close and hold her in your arms:
    Your anxious anxious face
Will tell her all as you return
    Upon the winds of space."

They wept and kissed: the waves were fringed
    With dancing dancing foam:
An old man leaned upon his stick
    And saw them safely home.

CLOSE ENCOUNTERS
OF THE SEVERN KIND

The year was 2020,
  And in the evening glow
Above the Devil's Chimney
  A spacecraft came in low.

It floated over Cheltenham
  Where all seemed calm and still;
It scanned the Golden Valley
  And circled Chosen Hill.

In search of warmth and friendship
  It came to earth and found
A cheering crowd and floodlights
  At Kingsholm rugby ground.

The aliens, emerging,
  Exhibited no fear,
Were clearly male and female
  And breathed our atmosphere.

Assured and diplomatic,
  They soon dispelled alarm
In slightly hesitant English
  Which possessed a certain charm.

They swiftly held a conference
  For all the media men,
And faced the candid camera
  And investigative pen.

Some questions were perceptive:
  "Did you pass the speed of light
Or slow the ageing process
  In interstellar flight?"

While some were more eccentric:
  "Have you heard of Captain Kirk?
Those circles in the cornfields -
  Are they your handiwork?"

While others were intrusive:
  "Have you heard of sex appeal?"
Or: "Tell us at this moment
  Exactly how you feel."

One spoke: "Your earthly notions
  Are simply out of phase":
The newsmen quickly noticed
  Her disenchanted gaze.

But others were more thoughtful:
  "You've flown across the years:
Please satisfy our longings
  And cure our mortal fears.

In your angelic orbit
  You've knocked at heaven's gate:
Is there a God above us,
  Or are we ruled by fate?

And do we have some freedom,
  Or is this just a play,
A stage, where our five senses
  Speak lines we have to say?

Are echoes in the darkness
  The voices of the dead?
Or is there just a silence,
  Our life a severed thread?"

They smiled: "We came to ask you
  These questions - every one.
We hoped that you could answer - ".
  The next day, they were gone.

CONJURER, ACTOR, TRICKSTER .....

I remember that night at the "Bird in Hand:
    The circle of friends, the quick applause,
The conjurer's patter, polished and bland,
    Sudden effect and hidden cause.

The ash on my unsuspecting palm
    Had passed through my hand, for all I knew;
His easy manner and tangible charm
    Almost persuaded me it was true.

He fingered the careworn, fortunate pack:
    "Now, for my magical coming-of-age" -
There lay the joker, the ten, and the Jack -
    "I shall graduate from the bar to the stage.

Sleight-of-hand has to take its turn;
    I shall begin my stage career
At the Music Hall - it's the place to learn;
    Come if you wish; you have nothing to fear.

Life, I'm told, can be unforgiving;
    (How many years at drama school?)
Out-of-work actors must still make a living;
    If it can't be Lear, I must play the Fool".

          *

"I present," said the compère, "a Knave of Hearts,
    A Lucifer, prince of legerdemain,
A Machiavelli of magical arts;
    Look for his secrets, but look in vain".

No doves , no cage, no lacquered box;
    He came with accessories pared to the bone;
No cards, no wand, no chains, no locks;
    A quick-change artist, he came alone.

In a crackle of lightning, Merlin appeared,
    Potent against an ancient power;
Faustus caressed his malevolent beard,
    Free from the Devil for one brief hour.

Joseph, clad in his coloured coat,
    Began to interpret the awkward dream;
Charon summoned the dead to float
    Across the subterranean stream.

A Pearly King with a flattened crown
    Swaggered in robes of sharp design;
Harlequin, tricked by the pallid Clown,
    Wept for ever for Columbine.

We knocked on the door of his changing-room
    Where the corridor came to a sombre end;
Only a candle relieved the gloom;
    We could not find our devious friend,

But only a shadow, enticed by fame,
    Who spoke in a whisper, remote and strange:
"I am Proteus, never the same;
    I am Chameleon: I change."

                *

An agent saw him; the lucky break
    That led to his first provincial role:
A part that he felt compelled to take
    In "Tinker, Tailor" - the Russian mole.

It met his need for concealed identity;
    Casting directors began to ask
For the hollow man, the divided entity,
    The actor trapped in a greasepaint mask.

A celebration; they heard him knock;
    No one enjoyed the Inspector's call;
All had been happy before the shock;
    Some were humbled after the fall.

He played the Alchemist, now entangled
    In roles that divided and multiplied;
He looked in mirrors, carefully angled;
    Some were true, but most of them lied.

Prospero summoned his latent powers,
    A prince concealed in a borrowed robe:
"Our revels are ended: the cloud-capped towers,
    The solemn temples, the imagined globe

Shall dissolve, and like this pageant fade:
    These our actors are melted into air,
The stuff of which our dreams are made,
    Visions harmonious and fair".

Finally, he was the modern magician,
    Summoning guests to his Grecian isle,
Striking a pose as the soul's physician,
    Smiling a bland, ironic smile.

"I apologise for some slight deception
    Practised upon your arrival here;
But I must remind you, truth is the exception;
    Things are seldom as they appear.

Even the evidence of the senses
    Can lull you into a foolish mistake;
This antique table, keeping up pretences,
    May in the end be a cunning fake.

Gaze for a time at the mutable ocean:
Opaque or transparent, jade or blue,
Tranquil or petulant: you have no notion
Which is the real, the definitive, hue.

Everything flows, for beyond the night
Lies daybreak: a shimmering lake of fire,
Like visual music, blurs the sight:
Apollo sings to a golden lyre.

I wait and watch on the rocky shore:
Night falls: the ancient god is dead:
An echoing emptiness at the core:
Alchemist's gold returned to lead.

All of us have altered since you came
By a metamorphosis, rich and strange:
I am Proteus, never the same:
I am Chameleon: I change."

*

Later, we tried to piece together
The steps that led to his slow decline;
The shifting breeze, the change in the weather,
The phase of the moon or the sinister sign.

Nobody seemed to be satisfied;
Perhaps that led to his fall from grace;
No one was able to step inside
The private life of the public face.

"A cardboard figure, hard to assess":
The critics glared at the vacant stage.
"Cold and hostile," announced the press,
Rather than print an empty page.

Later we found the methodical list
    Of those who had visibly failed to applaud,
And discovered in detail the final twist,
    The confidence trick or the company fraud.

The actor, chilled by his overdraft,
    Never found out whom he had to thank,
While his understudy quietly laughed
    All the way to the savings bank.

The croupier smiled as he sat apart,
    But the gossip-columnist had to leave,
Unaware that the missing heart
    Was hidden inside the expensive sleeve.

A fragile actress bequeathed her wealth,
    Signed away with a trembling pen
To the therapist who restored her health;
    Said that his name was Mr. Benn.

A plain-clothes officer set the trap:
    "I think we can give him a generous term";
But the only sound was the hesitant tap
    Of the man from the double-glazing firm.

He left his card by the window-frame:
    Then they noticed the writing, crabbed and strange:
"I am Proteus, never the same:
    I am Chameleon: I change".

*

Somewhere else, it might have been day.
    The river stirred in a leaden haze.
We broke the lock. The letters lay
    Dead, unopened. We entered the maze

17

And encountered a silence, so absolute
    That every sense seemed numbed and blurred
By the flitting movement, the sinuous route,
    The choking breath, the unspoken word.

The reticent months and the shifting seasons
    Became the uninformative years.
Elaborate theories and plausible reasons
    Turned in the end into simple fears.

                    *

The editor rang one day and said:
    "Here's a story I want you to cover;
Forget about 'Body in Garden Shed'
    And 'Councillor's Wife elopes with Lover'."

I followed the route, and came to a stop
    On the other side of the railway line,
In a crumbling street, by a tawdry shop:
    'CELESTIAL TOYMAKER' read the sign.

"An arrest is imminent": so it proved;
    I caught a glimpse of a blanketed shape.
Something about the way it moved
    Made me think of a conjurer's cape.

I looked in the window; some of the toys
    Were the stock-in-trade of practical jokers,
Cushions that made a dubious noise,
    Indelible inks and shocks for smokers.

I stepped inside; the shelves displayed
    Bases, liners, removing cream,
Crepe hair, sequins, taffeta, braid,
    Medals that shone with a spurious gleam.

Skeletons, puppets, marionettes,
    Hung like thieves on the wooden racks,
Vagrants paying their final debts
    With suspended heads and broken backs.

A peasant doll with a painted grin
    Opened, to show a doll that smiled;
Inside, an expressionless doll; within,
    The polished grain of a faceless child ....

.... SPY

He spoke at his trial: "I cannot deny
    That the evidence here is all you need:
Safe house, letterbox; courier, spy.
    Who did you blackmail to give you a lead?

Why was my incoming mail delayed?
    Who was the shadow with heavy feet?
But I still kept on with my export trade
    Till I saw you enter the one-way street.

Guilty, you say: am I to be tried
    By the cultured voice and the hooded glance?
You may keep your privilege, keep your pride;
    I will not join in your stately dance.

Guilty? A whispered word maintains
    The delicate poise of the dipping scales.
One country loses: another gains.
    Take away spies: the balance fails.

You call me guilty; so you suppose
    I could have travelled a different road?
This was the path I apparently chose;
    I could not break the genetic code.

Infant traumas, parental traits,
    Childhood fantasies shaped my soul;
Fixed, determined, set in my ways;
    Never the person, always the role.

Could I, in view of these various factors,
    Ever have acted otherwise?
Some of us, naturally, have to be actors;
    Some, inevitably, have to be spies.

No, I admit: there must be a time
    When the flexible man is free to choose
The compassionate act or the perfect crime,
    The open plan or the hidden ruse.

I am free; I am guilty; I am to blame:
    I realise you think my history strange;
But I am Proteus, never the same:
    I am Chameleon: I change."

[1982]

.... CROOK

He shuffled the cards as he spoke at his trial:
    "The evidence here is all you need;
I choose confession; no need for denial;
    For my last performance, I'll play the lead.

I was the dealer; who held the aces? -
    I offer the ten, the King, and the Jack -
The arms were hidden, and so were the faces;
    This was a game of defence and attack.

I tapped on the panels you had to move,
　　Showed you the papers behind the scenes,
Unlocked the cabinet, tried to prove,
　　That the end would justify the means.

So who am I now and who have I been?
　　Someone informed and somebody guessed:
Conjurer, actor or go-between:
　　Which of my masks did you like the best?

You call me guilty: but do you suppose
　　I could have travelled a different road?
This was the path I apparently chose;
　　How could I break the genetic code?

Infantile traumas, inherited traits,
　　Childhood fantasies shaped my soul;
Fixed, determined, set in my ways,
　　Never the person, always the role.

Could I , in view of these various factors,
　　Ever have acted otherwise?
Some of us, naturally, have to be actors,
　　Strangers to truth and friends to lies.

No, I admit: there must be a time
　　When the flexible man is free to choose
The compassionate act or the perfect crime,
　　The open plan or the hidden ruse.

I am free; I am guilty; I am to blame:
　　I realise you think my history strange:
But I am Proteus, never the same:
　　I am Chameleon: I change."

[1992]

THE MAZE

Our genes and chromosomes control our days,
Helped on by traumas and parental ties;
But we can find the centre of the maze.

We aim to compensate for all our traits,
Yet some of them are skulking in disguise
If genes and chromosomes control our days.

We think we know some truths, though in the haze
Of self-deception half of them are lies:
We try to find the centre of the maze.

We make decisions, yet at every phase
We ask: could we have acted otherwise
If genes and chromosomes control our days?

And all our better actions could be plays
Performed by our five senses for a prize:
But we can find the centre of the maze

And so acquire some independent ways.
We need to see ourselves with open eyes,
For genes and chromosomes control our days
Unless we find the centre of the maze.

AT THE LITERARY FESTIVAL

On a wet day in October
The witty but profound Czech poet
Met the serious and sensitive Russian poet
And an audience of three hundred people
In a large marquee.
The interior walls were decorated
With Austrian blinds
In order to give the proceedings
A post-totalitarian flavour
And to prevent the spectators feeling
That they were merely camping out.

There was a third voice.
A young actress with four young daughters
Safely at home
Read the Russian poems in translation
Thus enabling Irina Ratushinskaya
To be entirely herself.

There was also a fourth voice.
It was the anapaestic beat of motor cars
Giving way frequently
To the spondaic note of heavy lorries
In a totally unrehearsed performance
Just the other side of the canvas.

It makes the poetry more dramatic,
Said Miroslav Holub,
Thinking perhaps
Of more serious interruptions.

I did not agree at the time.
But when I look back
I have to believe him
Even if he did not intend me to do so.

For the traffic
Which over-acted so badly
In its unthinking attempt to distract us,
Merely threw into relief
The flow of Slavonic double and treble consonants
Rising and falling in the slightest variation
And speaking with the utmost poignancy
Of imprisonment and loss,
And the English voice with the Czech accent
Or simply the Czech voice
As it spoke of the moth
Which emerged from the pupa
But could not face its new found freedom.

And I realise now
That I only heard the traffic for ten minutes
But I heard the poetry
Outside my head
For a whole hour
And inside my head
I hear it now.

RALPH VAUGHAN WILLIAMS
(1872-1958)

They listened, in that cool, reflective place,
To music like the sweep of angels' wings,
Which moved with onward flow, or sudden pace,
And sang of pastoral or immortal things:
The lark ascending into cloudy space;
An older theme, spread on divided strings,
Which echoed, and possessed an arid grace;
A strident anthem for the King of Kings.

These cadences recall the tumbling mill,
The strands of folk-song, or the drover's rhyme;
One city deep below the troubled hill,
Another waking to the clock-tower's chime;
Or the celestial city, fair and still,
Where alleluias end the pilgrims' climb;
Or ice-bound falls and glaciers, which chill
The travellers' bones, and are the shrouds of time.

The sounds of war, and hymns for those who died,
Dissolve and fade: at sea, the breakers roll;
The sails and pennants fleck the ebbing tide;
Now, if some voyager to the unknown pole
Can find no comfort, no true map or guide,
But hears the muffled drums and dead bells toll,
And leaves the visible world unsatisfied,
Then let this music come, and flood his soul.

GUSTAV HOLST
1874-1934

Messenger
    With subtle wings,
Listen to
    These muted strings,
Visit us
    Without delay,
Tell us what
    The planets say.

My name is Saturn, bringer of old age:
    And I am Mars, who hastens war and death:
The runes and numbers cluster on the page,
    Invading chords that will not pause for breath
Until they form the prelude to a theme
    That starts its smooth ascent: fresh notes release
A waterfall of sound, a flowing stream:
    The evening star creates a mood of peace.

Open wide
    The cage's door,
Let the semi-
    Quavers soar,
Sparkle, scatter,
    Fall to earth,
Imitating
    Human mirth.

These changing moods are made of fire and ice:
    This symphony reflects the riverside,
The slow procession to the sacrifice,
    The priest, the sacred grove, the forest ride.
The old magician casts a brazen spell,
    Till incantations from the distant spheres
End in a wild glissando: all is well:
    This sudden resolution calms their fears.

        Trumpeter
          And perfect fool,
        Write the tunes
          We sang at school,
        Nearly, nearly
          Lost and gone,
        Ostinato,
          Dargason.

This hymn, this dance, reveals the maker's art,
    For drums and flutes repeat a plainsong air,
While words that shine through prisms move apart
    And merge in an intensity of prayer.
The alleluias falter in their flight:
    Neptune the mystic comes to take their place:
Arpeggios hang like tapestries of night
    And unseen voices interweave in space.

EDWARD ELGAR
1857-1934

Prologue

I write this music in my gratitude
To this sweet borderland where I have made
My home: the Malvern Hills, the woodland ways ...

C.A.E.

She married a craftsman,
Surveyed his letters,
Reviewed his bills,
Ruled his manuscripts,
Posted his scores,
Listened for the moment
When the silence would end
And the piano begin,
And know that another day's work
Was nearly done:
Spoke quietly:
Cared intensely:
Believed in him.

A.J.J.

Now you Englishmen
Have a composer at last,
You might be forgiven
For showing a little enthusiasm.
But oh no! It's only an English musician.
He's treated like a nobody.
He wrote me a letter: quite depressed:
But I told him: Look at the Pathétique Sonata:
That's the right mood for facing adversities.
Defy them!

D.P.

He played me a very odd tune:
Then some sketches
And some finished pieces.
I turned the pages:
We were serious, and laughed:
Then came a shock:
No. X. 'Dorabella'.
When it was over,
I could say nothing:
My mind in a whirl
Of pleasure, pride, and almost shame
That he should have written
Something so lovely about me.

H.J.W.

Quite extraordinary!
I had to play it again
With exactly the same result:
They simply refused to allow me
To get on with the rest of the programme:
Even when I brought on the soloist
Ready to sing 'Hiawatha'
They would not listen:
Merely to restore order
I played the march a third time:
The only double encore
In the entire history
Of the Promenade Concerts.

G.B.S.

Make the B.B.C.
Order a new symphony!
It can afford it:
A Financial Symphony.
Allegro: Impending Disaster.
Lento mesto: Stony Broke.
Scherzo: Light Heart and Empty Pocket.
Allegro: Clouds Clearing.

H.R.

One lives with one's regrets:
We were not ready for *The Dream.*
I sensed his disappointment
And did not make the same mistake again.
So the letter meant much to me:
Love and reverence ...
Greatest and most genuine friend.

Y.M.

He came to England:
Paused for a photograph
On the steps of the studios,
Age and youth together:
Released the secret soul
From its confinement:
Never forgotten.

K.F.

Singing without the score,
She faltered at the rehearsal:
A chance remark distressed her.
But she sang the Angel from memory,
Always .... always ....

T.E.L.

This is from my cottage.
Your second symphony
Gets further under our skins
Than anything else in the record library
At Clouds Hill.
Generally we play it last of all
Towards the middle of the night
Because nothing comes off very well after it.
One seems to stop there.

E.E.

I write this music in my gratitude
To this sweet borderland where I have made
My home: the Malvern Hills, the woodland ways:
And here I shall return, if it can be,
And move at leisure on these country paths.

I climb the Beacon,
Rest, and shade my eyes, and gaze
As far as the eye can see.
This is the chequered landscape of my life;
These winds that swirl around my head
Bring back a thousand memories
Of friendship, sadness, recognition;
And in the distance, voices.

We are the music makers,
And we are the dreamers of dreams ....

I went to sleep, and now I am refreshed ....

My life was as the vapour, and is not ....

.... And move at leisure on these country paths
That I have walked so many, many times.

This is my valediction.

CARL NIELSEN
1865-1931

Ten miles south of Odense
Where the shoemaker's son
Gazed at his miniature theatre
And dreamed of the little mermaid
Twelve children were born
To the house-painter and his wife.

The seventh child
Hammered on cordwood
Played in the village band
Went to the city to seek his fortune
And married a sculptress
With hair like wheat.

In the Royal Theatre
The two young lovers
Took off their masks
And danced to his music.

It was springtime on Fyn.
Far in the distance, wordless voices
Floated above the cornfields.
The sky darkened,
And the thunder began to reverberate.
Far out at sea the waves rose like black mountains
And the prince's ship dived down like a swan ...

The side-drummer was ordered to improvise
As if at all costs he wanted to stop
The progress of the orchestra.

... And rode up again on the towering crests ...

As if at all costs he wanted ...

... Half-drenched beneath the hammer blows ...

As if at all costs ...

And sailed across tumultuous seas
Out of the darkness, wings spread wide,
Traversing earth and heaven,
Unbroken, free, alive.

The steadfast tin soldier
Took no notice of the pain at his heart
And climbed the rope in the wings
At the end of the rehearsal.

Here stands his monument:
The Danish man
His hair like stubble
Astride a wild horse.

JEAN SIBELIUS (1865-1957)

Kalevala
Karelia

                                              white
                                              green
                                              copper
                                              gold

              water
              flesh
              willows
              grass

Karelia
Kalevala

              Vainamoinen
              Son of the sea
              And Ilmatar daughter of air
              Asked for the hand .
              Of Aino the graceful

                                              white and green
                                              copper and gold

              She would not marry
              But swam to a rock
              That broke into pieces
              And as she drowned
              She was transformed
              Blood into water
              Flesh into fish
              Ribs into willows
              Hair into sea grass

                                        forests of pine
                                        green and black
                                        travelling north
                                        to the land of the dead
                broke into pieces

Finlandia
Karelia
                she was transformed
                                        music of shadows
                                        oboes and horns
                                        hollow and sombre
                                        tunnels of sound
                hair into sea grass
                                        ice and fire
                                        white and gold

Karelia
Finlandia
                Vainamoinen
                Flew to the north
                On an eagle's back
                And on his return
                Looked up to see
                Pohjola's daughter
                Deftly spinning
                Aloft on a rainbow
                He asked for her hand
                But the tasks she set
                Were beyond his powers

Kalevala
Karelia
                                        clouds reflected
                                        in still blue lakes

When Lemminkainen
Companion and hero
Asked for her hand
He was commanded
To kill with one arrow
The sacred swan
Of Tuoni the river
That flows between
The land of the living
And the land of the dead.

Tuonela
Tapiola

the cold wind slides
through the forests of pine

He drew his bow
But was cut into fragments
And borne on the river
Through leaves of ice

strings like sinews
plucked and fingered
scattering sound
like flakes of snow

His grieving mother
Restored him to life
And made him whole
With her magical songs

Tapiola
Tuonela

water to blood
fish into flesh
willows to ribs
seagrass to hair

shadows and sunlight
tundra and forest

So Vainamoinen
Set out to travel
To the north once more
And killed a pike
Which he cut into fragments
Making a kantele
Out of the bones
An intricate harp
Only he could play

Kalevala
Finlandia

                                        white and gold
                                        ice and fire

And as his fingers
Ran over the strings
The phrases he formed
Were shafts of sunlight
Melting the ice
On the still blue lakes
Splintering shadows
Deep in the forest
Stirring the echoes
Of horns and trumpets
Hollow and sombre
Rising and falling
Dissolving the snow
Setting fire to the air
Till all creatures listened
And all men wept

And when he was old
He sailed away
In a copper boat
Into the west
Singing his wonderful songs

GASPARD DE LA NUIT

In that cold climate, night fell like a veil:
There, at the misty edge of the inhabited world,
I dropped at once into exhausted sleep.

A tiny creature, like a bat, uncurled,
Spread out its parchment wings, and with its claws
Clung to the tattered curtains of my mind;
Then launched into the quick and giddy flight
Of bright hallucination's quick despair:
Scarbo, Flibbertigibbet, Fly-by-Night
Clattered in agitation on the air.
I reached out hands to throttle it, and choke
Its gasping breath: I snatched and caught ...
                              I woke:
The birch tree stood beneath the winter moon;
Its branches brushed the roof without a pause.

Clear on the skyline, gazing into space,
A dead man on a gallows spun life's thread:
I watched, obsessed: then, with reluctant tread
And flickering heart-beat, stumbled in a trance
To contemplate that spinning, murderous dance.
The hands were knotted. "Will *your* death be soon?"
The bent back asked; then turned.
                              I saw my face.

I woke. The birch-tree arched against the hail.

Her face was wet with raindrops, or with tears,
Or river-water: beautiful and free,
Her black hair hid her cheek, as if to keep
Her love beyond my reach: all I could find
In deep dreams was fulfilment of my fears.

I woke; and she was leaning over me:
And I - fool, poet, traveller, what you will -
Gave her my hand and, feverless, lay still.

LEGENDS

Cry sorrow, sorrow, but let good prevail.

> *Aeschylus: Agamemnon*

Love, unconquerable ...

> *Sophocles: Antigone*

Love will survive, although the heart may fail:
Once, Oedipus gave way to rage and lust:
Cry sorrow, sorrow, but let good prevail.

His daughters cared for him, though old and frail,
Whose eyes had felt the jewelled needle's thrust:
Love will survive, although the heart may fail.

The battle seared the city like a gale:
Their brother perished, though his cause was just:
Cry sorrow, sorrow, but let good prevail.

His sister wept and stole outside the pale
To scatter on his corpse the sacred dust:
Love will survive, although the heart may fail.

Two brothers and their skilful friend set sail
For Troy, to kill the prince they could not trust:
Cry sorrow, sorrow, but let good prevail.

One wife planned murder, as her life grew stale:
The other waited, as all true wives must:
Love will survive, although the heart may fail:
Cry sorrow, sorrow, but let good prevail.

KINGS AND PRINCES

The colonnades and pillars
    Enclose the palace door:
The angled stair stabs downwards
    Past the dancing-floor.

The frescoes in the courtyard
    Reflect the torches' blaze:
The hostages from Athens
    Penetrate the maze,

And through caves and cellars
    Hesitantly tread,
Their prince and leader clutching
    The dagger and the thread.

The Minotaur pursues them,
    But Theseus wins the race
And finds beneath the bull mask
    The twisted human face

Of the son and heir of Minos:
    So the debt is paid at last
By those who sail for Athens
    With the black sail at the mast.

But Ariadne's weeping
    On Naxos in despair,
And the white sail is forgotten
    By a prince who does not care

That a promise has been broken,
    And now must take the blame
For his royal father's drowning
    In the sea that bears his name.

RUSKIN AT BRANTWOOD

The *Gondola* glides down the lake;
Its ripples filter far and wide;
On Coniston, the steamer's wake
Creates the shadow of a tide.

The stones of Venice, clear as light,
Were pictured by his artist's hand;
The seven lamps, precise and bright,
Inspired a dry Victorian land.

He came to scan these wooded slopes,
But woke too soon, drew back the blind,
And nursed his long extinguished hopes
And storms that swept across his mind.

The lake is still; the sails are furled.
I look at Brantwood, white and pure,
Think less of books that change the world
And more of those that heal and cure,

And wish he'd found a way to dream
And sleep and rest and mend the heart.
The *Gondola's* a wisp of steam;
The painted lake a work of art.

THE RIEVAULX TERRACE

Above the woods
   A sudden space
A calm expanse
   A quiet place

A shallow arc
   A gentle bend
You cannot see
   From end to end

A width of grass
   An archer's bow
A scarp that meets
   The vale below

Orchid and cowslip
  Fringe the hill
Organic life
  Where all is still

At north and south
  A temple stands
Twin miniatures
  By artists' hands

A stroll reveals
  The Tuscan dome
A Grecian frieze
  The pillars, Rome

Austere design
  Of woven rings
Alone, a goddess
  Spreads her wings

Ionic temple
  Open doors
Olympus on
  The Yorkshire moors

Above, Apollo
  Wakes the dawn
The Muses tread
  The painted lawn

While Venus trades
  In sulky charms
Imprisoned by
  Dark Vulcan's arms

Below, a Georgian
    Table spread
For mortal meat
    And mortal bread

Like Atlases
    Twin eagles hold
Siena marble
    Fringed with gold

While face to face
    Two sphinxes crouch
Confined beneath
    A gilded couch

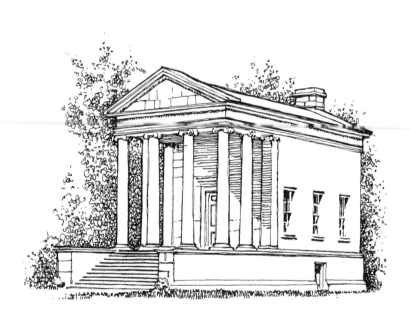

A depth below
   These sculptured toys
The abbey stands
   In equipoise

The precinct frames
   The ruined nave
A skeleton
   Without a grave

Monastic life
   That petrified
And froze, before
   Its buildings died

The pagan gods
   Endured our fates
Unruly loves
   Disordered hates

Though Plato scorned
   Their human ways
Too much like ours
   For blame or praise

Some know a God
   Who came to earth
And shared the sorrows
   Of our birth

For Him we climb
   The hillside, where
The terrace floats
   As if on air.

NORTHUMBRIA

Enter this hot-air balloon
And climb to seagull-height:
This coastline now must seem
Like bands of green and gold and blue,
A banner for the storm-swept ancient kingdom:
Or an apple-green bishop's mantle
With costly embroidered fringe
Laid out upon an altar-cloth
That's close to Mary's colouring.
Look down again: these twisted ornaments,
Formed by the craftsman's art,
Are all that's left of castles:
Berwick, Alnwick, Bamburgh, Dunstanburgh.
This clasp upon the mantle,
Linked by a slender chain,
Is the Holy Island of Lindisfarne,
Where Aidan built his church and monastery
And the Gospels, scrolled in Celtic colours,
Green and gold and delicate blue,
Took shape and glowed on the lectern.
Descend, descend: these dark motifs,
Spread on the altar-cloth like a broken rosary,
Are the Farne Islands, home for hermits and birds,
Where Longstone's lighthouse-keeper
And his daughter rowed in a coble
To reach the *Forfarshire* and save eight souls.
Come down to earth at Bamburgh:
Here is Grace Darling's tomb
Close to St. Aidan's Church,
Still within sight of the sea.

Here where two lanes converge,
Past the comfortable tea-rooms
And the well-kept cricket pitch,
The crenellated battlements stand firm
And guard this sweep of sand.
Here on a Sunday morning
We walked like other silhouettes,
Watchers upon the shore,
Looking at sea and sky
As if to find life's meaning,
Feeling a measure of faith.

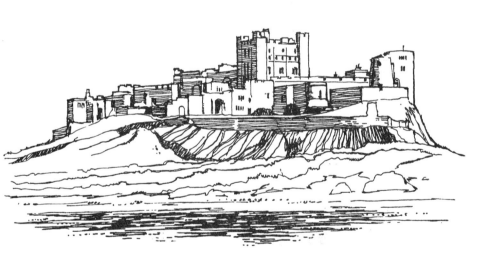

A LETTER TO MY DAUGHTER

Galileo and his daughter exchanged many letters;
hers survive and appear in Dava Sobel's book;
his have never been found.

Most pious daughter, Maria Celeste,
Bestowed by her father on her mother, the Church,
I pray that you will forgive me
For my undoubted procrastination
In writing to you of the judgement.
I have to confess that stillness of soul
Eluded me, so that for several days
I could not rest, or sleep, or even pray.
I hoped against hope that the matter would end
In common accord, in a form of words
Whereby we should all be reconciled:
But, as you now know, the verdict was harsh.
Yes, the " Dialogue" has been condemned
And I must abandon the erroneous theories
That say that the earth moves round the sun:
And thus the matter has been resolved.
The Inquisition has enjoined me further
To recite the penitential psalms:
I am a prisoner, suspected of heresy.
His Holiness has indeed shown mercy
And let me quit Rome for Siena
Where I am held by the kindest of gaolers.
I can hope, I can only live in hope
That this is a step to Arcetri:
That we may one day be close again
Though the walls of the convent divide us.
And be consoled, my dearest daughter:
I shall sleep: I shall rest: I shall pray.
For we ascertain from the Gospels
That some were cured in an instant
When our Lord was close at hand,

But we who are distant from Him in time
Must live by the parable and persevere;
So the intercessions of which you write
Together with mine will climb to Heaven.
My daughter, you have the healing power
Bestowed by our Lord upon his disciples.
Your words are a medicine to me.
I enclose the three scudi you requested
For the purchase of herbs for Sister Luisa.
I entreat you, destroy my letters,
For since the heretic has not been burnt,
His writings must take his place.

*

HUBBLE

They fell to earth. Their mission was complete:
To fix, by means of casual walks in space,
Corrective optics lightly in their place,
And leave the craft in order, trim and neat.

Kaleidoscopic patterns met their gaze:
The pixels focussed into wheels of fire,
New stars created, or the funeral pyre
Of supernovas in their final phase.

In time they found the unsuspected moons
That drift round Saturn: as the dusks and noons
Denied them sleep, Orion built his towers
Of cloudy fragments: so they spent the hours,
And breathed again, and saw to their relief
The whole galactic forest, tree and leaf.

THE CLOCKMAKER'S CAROL

A stained glass window in St George's Church, Tuffley,
Gloucester, depicts the infant Jesus holding an apple.
This comes from an Austrian legend, which is told here.

Every year a child was found,
  Gifts for each December made:
Customs kept since clocks were wound,
  Practised by each guild and trade:
    Shopkeeper, carpenter, cook with her ladle,
    Ready to kneel at the little one's cradle.

Every toy was made to please,
  Polished by the craftsman's art:
Cups and tables, locks and keys,
  Gift and maker had to part:
    Pottery, crockery, bricklayer's wall,
    The clockmaker's clock was the best of them all.

But one day his solid door
  Felt the Burgomaster's knock:
"That is mine!" "But I'm too poor,
  Sir, to make another clock."
    Close by the apple-tree, icicles harden;
    Snow softly falls in the clockmaker's garden.

Still he went to see the child,
  Took a gift of lesser cost:
But the tiny baby smiled,
  Held the apple, touched the frost.
    Dance on the rooftops and dance in the air;
    The clockmaker's hands are enfolded in prayer.

BEYOND THE HORIZON

This is the country of facts,
And there, beyond the horizon,
Lies the country of fiction.
Between them lies a borderland;
I'd call it no man's land,
But many people live there.
Set out upon your journey,
Starting with the truth.
It is a fact you cannot tell
When you have reached the border;
You'll only know when you've arrived.
These friendly faces are serial actors,
Their characters asked for advice,
Sent gifts when they fall ill.
Here is scandal and revelation;
Read the versions in all the papers,
Alternative lives of alternative people.
Watch out for marauding bands
Who damage the truth;
They call them factions.
The heat-haze rises,
A mirage forms;
Climb to the skyline, and descend.
Against all expectations,
The air is clear and cool.
Here is the land of story and fable,
Here is the land of myth and dreaming,
Of ordinary and extraordinary lives
Enhanced, transformed, interpreted
By the force of the imagination.
Wherever we are, this country calls us;
We long to be there.

ARCADIA

The landscape of Arcadia
    Can change before your eyes,
For its contours are subjective
    And its element, surprise.

The clearing in the forest
    Dissolves in summer air,
As a naiad by the lakeside
    Reveals her auburn hair;

Or the subtle surf is curling
    On the Polynesian shore,
Where coral castles waver
    Above the ocean floor;

Or outback fades to desert
    And dunes of trembling sand
Where the blue and gold horizon
    Conceals the promised land.

But isolated crofters
    Must till an arid soil,
And happy pastoral poems
    Idealise their toil,

And girls that Gauguin painted
    Have different goods to sell,
For sweet Miranda's island
    Housed Caliban as well,

And the boy who trod the songlines
    And became the exiles' guide
Contracted their infection,
    Lay down, and quietly died.

So that we should surrender
    Our wish to travel there,
Relinquish to Arcadia
    Its thin untroubled air,

And keep within a country
    Whose borders are confined,
And leave intact for ever
    These Edens of the mind.

*

GARDEN HAIKU

The Japanese quince
Displays its scarlet rosettes
Awarded to spring.

Japanese iris
Like splinters of sun and sky
Shelters by the wall.

Japanese anenome
Painted white or pink
By unseen artist.

Japanese maple
Lights bonfire of crimson leaves,
Sets autumn ablaze.

The bonsai gardener
Nurtures his family tree -
Ancestor worship.

UNDER WATER

We lived in water once: our supple skins,
Our flowing hair and limbs, the way we dance,
Provide the evidence: we passed an age
In that aquatic world. Recalled to land,
We hunted, gathered, settled, looked like men.
Only our twists and tumbles in the dark
Reminded us that once we swam: at birth
We wept ....
       Still cry ....
              Salt water hurts our eyes.
We die by drowning. Silent homes have died,
Their timbers parted by the drenching tide;
But as we watch and listen on the strand,
We hear their voices, feel they are alive,
Or oceanic music calls to mind
The Breton city, flooded for its sins,
Whose people sense, like footsteps in a dream,
The carillon that summons them to prayer
In pentatonic timbres set to chime
In unseen changes past the reach of time.

A breeze disturbs the waves' serenity;
Orchestral rhythms curl upon the shore.
The sea awakes; its contours are defined.
The liquid sun emerges from the haze
And spills the molten metal from its core.
So when the ice-caps thaw, the oceans rise,
The tropics start their limitless advance,
The sweltering jungles form a tangled arc
Around each bay and unexpected firth,
Familiar sights are islands in the stream,
And earth gives way to water, shall we dive

Into those depths, and live and die again
Beyond the bars of this terrestrial cage?

I do not wish my bones to lie so deep,
But if there is a cemetery by the sea
Between the pines, where I can rest and gaze
And listen to the hymn of waves and air,
That is the place where I would like to sleep.

AN UNEVENTFUL WORLD

I know there is an uneventful world
Where patient Orpheus does not turn his head,
But steals Eurydice from among the dead,
Theseus, returning, keeps the black sails furled,
The Capulets receive the happy pair,
Iseult and Tristan sail to Lyonesse,
And, in a country farmhouse, blissful Tess
Waits on a loving and forgiving Clare.

I realise: those writers who believe in fate
Would leave at once in evident confusion;
Those too, whose occupation is intrustion
Into our private lives, the Fourth Estate;
But some, perhaps, would take a different view:
How commonplace this world is, and how true.

A SPELL

Duntisbourne Abbots
And Duntisbourne Leer:
A spell for healing,
A charm for fear.

Duntisbourne (Middle)
And Duntisbourne Rouse:
A garland of names
To protect the house.

Walk and walk,
And you're sure to find
A simple cure
For the fretting mind,

And a Cotswold walk
Will make you whole
And bring some calm
To the restless soul.

Duntisbourne Abbots,
And Duntisbourne Leer:
The stream flows on
And the air is clear.

Duntisbourne (Middle)
And Duntisbourne Rouse:
There's straw in the barn
And a cat with a mouse.

Three good friends
(And it's sometimes four)
Follow the path
On the valley floor.

Some people we know
Take a humorous line,
And mention "The Last
Of the Summer Wine".

This isn't the Dales
Or the Cleveland Way,
But there could be something
In what they say,

For we turn the corner
And climb the hill,
There's an autumn sun
And the air is still,

And it's time to pause
For a bite and a drink,
A place with a view
And a time to think

That however often
We cover the miles
Down country lanes,
Through gates and stiles,

There will always be,
While the ages run,
One more village
Asleep in the sun,

With window boxes
And mellow stones
And a place of rest
For travellers' bones:

Duntisbourne End
Or Somewhere Leer:
Search on the map,
It will disappear.

But walk and walk
And you'll find it there
Caught in the spell
Of the autumn air,

Where no one, it seems,
Could come to harm:
A dovecot, an orchard,
An inn and a farm,

And a Saxon church
And a manor house:
Duntisbourne Anywhere:
Nowhere Rouse.

ONCE UPON A TIME

The Gloucester-Sharpness Canal

Ports are open, locks are new,
Goods are set to travel through,
       Waters, waters,
       Waters flow.

Towpath runs a steady course
For the boatman and his horse,
       Plodding, plodding,
       Plodding slow.

Wives and children, fears and hopes,
Painted cabins, knotted ropes:
       Pretty, pretty,
       Pretty show.

Cargo boat from Severnside,
Safe from sand and safe from tide,
       Heavy, heavy,
       Heavy trow.

Stately brig and brigantine,
Ocean king and ocean queen,
       Dipping, dipping,
       Dipping low.

Journey's end, a welcome sight:
Gloucester in the evening light:
       Sunset, sunset,
       Sunset glow.

These are phantoms of the past,
Ghostly sail and ghostly mast,
       All we, all we,
       All we know.

STEAM TEAS

From Chepstow up to Monmouth
    The twisting railway ran;
It spluttered through the woodland,
    It crossed a single span,

And paused for breath at Tintern
    Where calmly flows the Wye
From Brockweir and Llandogo
    Beneath a border sky.

And *you* can stop at Tintern;
    The station's selling snacks,
There are crafts instead of tickets
    And lawns instead of tracks,

And stock that's finished rolling,
    With souvenirs for sale:
A reason to remember
    The distant days of rail.

From Aberdeen to Ballater
    The royal railway strolled
To cosset Queen Victoria
    And keep her from the cold.

The Dee ran swiftly onwards
    In clouds of silver spray
And funnelled past the stations
    That lined the impermanent way.

There's tea and scones at Ballater
    (You'll find an open door);
There's turf instead of ballast
    And heather on the moor;

And on these sunlit platforms
    You can cogitate and dream,
And listen in your memory
    To the vanished sounds of steam.

THE SCULPTURE TRAIL

Royal Forest of Dean

At Beechenhurst
    The path divides,
And as you walk
    The forest rides

You come across
    A sculptured chair,
A window floating
    In mid-air,

A headstone for
    A long-lost mine,
Carved sleepers for
    A railway line,

A house on stilts,
    A crown of fire,
A mound that forms
    A funeral pyre.

But some have merged
    With soil and leaf,
Their stay intended
    To be brief.

These wicker deer
    That crossed the pond
Have vanished in
    The woods beyond.

So they, like us,
    Decay and fall:
The quiet trees
    Outlive us all.

GLOUCESTER

The Roman legions settled by the stream;
A Saxon queen imposed her father's plan.
The Normans came; the Domesday Book began;
The solid nave fulfilled the abbot's dream.
A golden circlet served to crown a king;
Here, pilgrims flocked to see their murdered liege.
The roundhead army came to raise the siege;
The congregations heard the three choirs sing.

This city has no walls, no keep, no cross:
Few timbers still remain: when all else fails,
It must rebuild, or excavate, or comb
The records for each unexpected loss.
It clings to history by its fingernails,
Tries hard to please its guests, and feels like home.

GLOUCESTER:
AN UNRELIABLE HISTORY

This first verse takes a cursory view,
    So let me turn the pages
Past Stone Age, Old and Middle and New,
    Past Bronze and Iron Ages,

Till the Romans came to a Channel port,
    Then out to Severn strode,
Down Ermin Street to Kingsholm fort
    By way of London Road.

They brought the tribesmen under their thumb
    With the tortoise or "testudo":
It was closer to a rugby scrum
    Than a friendly game like ludo.

The twentieth legion came to a halt,
    Settled and made a home,
Though the veterans still kept finding fault:
    No place, they said, like Rome.

They watched, and kept the Welsh at bay;
    Guard duties seemed eternal;
They read, to pass the time of day,
    The "Citizen" and "Journal".

In Eastgate Street, where trowel and spade
    Have uncovered the city's roots,
A chain store did a lively trade:
    Caligulas, or Boots.

The Romans left; now the Saxons saw
    Three townships in their path,
And made them keep King Osric's law:
    That's Glevum, Ciren, Bath.

But the Danes retreated to swamp and fen
    Afraid of a female leader:
Queen Boadicea rides again -
    The Lady Aethelflaeda.

She fitted the town for future wars
    With timber, stones and mortar,
Neglecting her domestic chores
    (She *was* King Alfred's daughter).

The citizens found it a fearful wrench
    To kneel to a Norman King:
They had to brush up their Latin and French
    And forget all their Early Eng.

And so the Domesday Book was sealed;
    The King went to his grave,
And never saw, on Osric's field,
    The Abbey's choir and nave.

A change of mood, which you may fault:
    But the monks were mortified
When the cloisters went up, vault by vault,
    On the north, or shady side.

A wall enclosed the monastic piece;
    The gates were firm and sound;
So they went in search of the "Ram" and "Fleece"
    By burrowing underground.

They say Dick Whittington lived in this house,
    Or perhaps it was just his cat;
Well, they found the skeleton of a mouse;
    You can be sure of that.

Now Henry VIII, to grant a boon,
    Took Anne to a royal meet;
They ate their meals with a wooden spoon
    In the hospitality suite.

A serious verse: now stand and pause
    Before St. Mary's Gate;
John Hooper stood for the common cause
    And met with a fiery fate.

A learned doctor came and went;
    They say his name was Foster.
Take my word; Sir Nathaniel Brent
    Was the lawyer who came to Gloucester.

War came: the Puritans barred the gates
    And disobeyed their liege,
Paid a commander out of the rates,
    And settled for a siege.

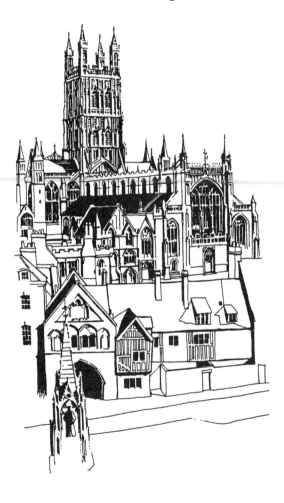

The Earl of Essex brought relief;
    The rhymes they wrote were witty,
Humpty Dumpty coming to grief,
    Or the pig that saved the city.

But then the walls came tumbling down;
    For stubborn Gloucester folk,
The Restoration of the town
    Became some kind of joke.

The railways arrived: the docks decayed:
    No time for spars and sails.
Here's James Onedin, ready-made:
    He'll do when all else fails.

The Jellicoe Plan came into play
    To relieve our sense of guilt,
With the Via Sacra, or Sacred Way,
    Or history rebuilt.

They planned to construct the Inner Ring
    Around the edge of the Park,
But recession put a stop to the thing,
    So they called it the Inner Arc.

But before the redevelopment wars
    Could reduce the city to dust,
A meeting of friends in Southern's Stores
    Created the Civic Trust.

This city has no walls, no cross,
    No gates, no castle keep,
Few timbers now: each painful loss
    Would make stone faces weep.

But some still guard, or even love,
    Its scarred and human face.
I think the angels glide above
    This home: this time-worn place.

THE TRUE STORY OF DOCTOR FOSTER

There is a Gloucestershire tradition that Doctor Foster was a representative of William Laud, Archbishop of Canterbury, who was sent on a tour to put church matters in order There is plenty of evidence for this event, but no mention of anyone with that name. However, there may be an explanation

Many held as true
The Puritan view
And did not wish to falter:
That a cloth could be spread
For the Breaking of Bread
On a table instead of an altar.

But William Laud
Thought this was a fraud,
And moved his Communion table
To its former site
(Which he thought was right)
As soon as he was able.

Archbishop at last,
He now held fast
That the whole of the English nation
Should be brought to heel
(Not sit, but kneel)
By means of a new visitation.

A Reverend man
With a suitable plan
For keeping tradition alive,
Sir Nathaniel Brent
To Gloucester went
In sixteen thirty-five.

A Doctor of Law,
He allowed no flaw
In the pleading of different causes:
Each priest and clerk
Must make his mark
On a list of thirteen clauses.

But unseasonal rains
And a shortage of drains
Left the doctor soaked to the waist:
His superior smile
Disappeared for a while:
Such matters were not to his taste.

And the water and mud
Of the river in flood
Cut *one* village off from the town:
So Deerhurst Church
Was left in the lurch:
Neither lawyer nor vicar need drown.

So Puritan folk
Who thought it a joke,
For they scorned both Church and State,
Invented some verses
(Much better than curses)
About his unfortunate fate.

But walls had ears,
And people had fears
Of courts in the city of Gloucester,
And instead of Brent
(They knew who they meant)
They borrowed the name of Foster.

By eighteen-ten
Some studious men
Had gathered some nursery rhymes,
In miniature writing,
So very inviting
For the children of those times.

The elegant house
Of Francis Douce
Was the home for Bodley's books,
While Joseph Ritson
Fastened his wits on
Verses in crannies and nooks.

"Gammer Gurton's Garden" -
I beg your pardon,
Garland's the word I need -
Has the following feature,
"The Sedate Preacher",
And these are the words you can read.

"Old Doctor Forster
Went to Glo'ster
To preach the Word of God.
When he came there
He sate in his chair
And gave all the people a nod."

And thirty years later,
Another collator
(James Halliwell, I believe)
Published *this* ditty,
Precise and pretty,
From folk with a tale to weave.

"Doctor Foster
Came to Gloucester
In a shower of rain.
He stepped in a puddle
Right up to his middle
And never went there again."

You may have supposed
That the case is closed
And the story sunk without trace,
But there's truth in the fable,
And Deerhurst table
Still stands in the holy place.

TROY: THE FACTS

The battle stilled: the Greeks withdrew
    Across the ringing plain.
The walls of Troy stood firm and true:
    The siege had been in vain.

"Accept this gift," the traitor said :
    "We're on our homeward course,
But, mindful of your noble dead,
    We leave this wooden horse."

The Trojans pranced around the steed;
    Their bards were wise and witty;
They dragged it with unthinking greed
    Into their windy city.

Inside the horse, as Troy gave thanks,
    The Greeks began to yawn,
Peered through the cracks between the planks,
    And waited for the dawn.

Their leader, on the final shift,
    Observed the break of day:
Then found the trapdoor would not lift
    And cried out in dismay:

"The trap is fixed; we cannot win;
    For there can be no doubt
A double agent brought us in
    But will not let us out."

The Greek fleet, which that night had lurked
    Near Tenedos, now sailed
Inshore, in case the plan had worked,
    To find that it had failed.

The Trojans staged a grateful rite,
  Began the funeral games,
And swiftly set the beast alight
  With sacrificial flames.

The Greeks regained their craggy shore
  Determined to pretend
That those who would return no more
  Had reached a fitting end.

"No smoke," they said, "without a fire,"
  (Some licence was allowed):
"The citadel became a pyre:
  "We left beneath a cloud."

The legend grew: "Troy bit the dust;
  We razed it to the soil:
A suitable reward, we trust,
  For more than ten years' toil."

Across the sea, the traitor earned
  King Priam's accolade,
But, shamed in public, quickly learned
  The price that must be paid;

While Paris and Helen passed the hours
  Exchanging smile for smile,
And sunbathed on the topless towers
  In the Minoan style.

So nine proud cities stood and fell,
  Till Heinrich Schliemann found
The one of which the legends tell
  Beneath the Turkish mound.

But time and dust can soon conceal
  A city's ancient glory:
So, for our readers, we reveal:
  TROY - THE AUTHENTIC STORY.

THE COMPUTER'S FIRST DIARY

Monday: journey from the docks,
Stifled in a cardboard box:
Little time for dates and clocks:
I'm too fragile for these shocks.

Tuesday:switched on: feeling blue,
Though it is my normal hue:
Still, I have a super view
Through my two way V.D.U.,

And my maker in his guile,
Smiling a reclusive smile,
Packaged an internal file
So that I could write in style.

Wednesday: hope I will be sold:
Demonstration leaves me cold:
I've a story to unfold:
Eighty megabytes is gold.

Some of it must go on DOS:
Some on Windows: that's my loss:
Any more would make me cross:
I write diaries, not dross.

Thursday: it is as I feared:
Now my screen has almost cleared:
My new owner has appeared:
Something tells me he is weird.

Life is hard: he cannot cope:
He is boredom: I am hope:
He's the viewer: I'm the soap:
He's the addict: I'm the dope.

Friday: he's been up since four,
Filling up my disc to store
Applications by the score:
I can't take them any more:

Programmes with outlandish names:
Funny fonts and ghastly games:
Will I be the one he blames
If I just go up in flames?

Saturday: this is obscene:
To call a halt, I must be mean:
So I print in shades of green
An error message on the screen:

"Insufficient private space:
Please delete your database:
Go and join the human race:
P.S. I do not like your face."

Sunday morning, clear and bright:
Here's his answer: "You are right:
You have given me a fright,
But thanks to you I've seen the light.

I'll read the papers, watch the news;
Talk to folks with different views;
Walk the hills, disperse the blues;
Write some poems, hear the Muse."

Monday: time to turn the page:
No more calculated rage:
I've unlocked his mental cage:
He's the pupil: I'm the sage.

He is clearly on the mend:
An hour a day, and that's the end:
We've begun another trend:
He's the user: I'm the friend.

GARDEN WARS

There was trouble in the garden;
    There was trouble underground;
For the hideous force of evil
    Lay in wait without a sound.

There was trouble in the border,
    For everywhere I dug
Were the pestilential allies
    Of the fierce Invader Slug.

His troops were moulds and aphids
    And snails and worms and weeds,
And instead of X-wing fighters
    He had dandelion seeds;

And as his battle station
    He held the Compost Heap,
And there throughout the winter
    He'd bide his time and sleep.

But in the vernal season
    (That's spring, if you're not sure),
He'd mobilise his troopers
    And feed them on manure;

Then send them on their mission:
    To cultivate a taste
For vegetable ruin
    And horticultural waste.

There was Spittle Bug and Canker,
    There was Codlin Moth and Thrip,
There were Sawflies and Leaf Miner
    That could munch and chew and nip.

There was Black Spot and Botrytis
  And Mealy Bug and Scab;
There were chafer bugs and beetles
  That could masticate and grab.

Well, I should have told you earlier,
  Luke Gardener's my name;
I'm young and inexperienced;
  I'm really not to blame

If the garden's like a desert
  Of sodium-yellow sand,
Where double suns in orbit
  Bleach a parched, infertile land.

But I could not fail or falter
  For that would be a crime,
So I listened on the satellite
  To "Gardeners' Question Time";

And I wrote and asked The Chairman
  With his lethal laser beam,
To help me find the aliens
  And make them squirm and scream;

And two metallic robots
  Came humming to our aid,
As we turned to electronics
  To replace the fork and spade.

We patrolled the kitchen garden
  And the flower-beds, in pairs,
To spot their hiding-places
  And infiltrate their lairs.

We hunted in the hedgerows
  In sun and wind and rain:
We prowled around the pathways
  And patios - in vain.

So The Chairman took for safety
  A scarab beetle's case,
And swore he'd find Invader
  And meet him face to face.

He dug deep in the compost,
  Half-stifled by the stench,
When suddenly Invader
  Reared upright from the trench.

The breath screen kept his features
  Still hidden from our view,
And his sabre pierced The Chairman
  And split him into two.

Now I keep to country customs,
  So I built a funeral pyre,
And I stood there in the twilight
  As the flames grew ever higher.

I scattered all the ashes
  Near the furrow where he'd stood,
And I have to say, the roses
  Have never been so good.

So I rummage in the woodshed
  For the trowel and the hoe,
And renew my resolution
  To seek the horrid foe.

But I've made some sound investments,
  For lead can turn to gold,
And there's cash in fertilisers,
  And remedies for mould;

And they're going to make a movie,
  For that's where the profits are;
Called "Battleship Gardenia" -
  Just guess who'll be the star.

FIRST THINGS FIRST

She was a Guide, and he was a Scout;
   They played in a marching band.
The time for parade slipped by as they strolled
   Through the fairground, hand in hand.

They stopped for a while by the Penny Falls;
   They paused by the coconut shies;
He gazed through a fringe of candy floss
   Into her hazel eyes.

The reckoning came the following day:
   His leader's voice was stern:
"This is no way to be prepared;
   There are lessons you have to learn.

Girls don't exist; you must stay with the troop
   As a Cub must hunt with the pack.
Remember the hat with the broad flat brim,
   And follow the old straight track.

How do you think the Mafeking men
   Would have come to grips with the Boer
If their minds had been on the girls back home
   Instead of their semaphore?

Take some advice from me, young man;
   I can claim to be well versed
In the Laws and the Promises life demands:
   Always put first things first."

She stood, head bowed, while her captain gave
   A sentence that seemed severe:
"You must join a different company,
   And give up the band, my dear.

The pioneer guides had to 'ride and swim,
  Climb a tree and track a man';
But I think you have misinterpreted
  The aims of that early plan.

I should concentrate on your Homemaker badge
  And not on your clarinet;
If you make this sacrifice now" - and she smiled -
  "Be sure he'll never forget.

There are trees to be planted, fires to be lit,
  Children who need to be nursed;
Take my advice, for it's kindly meant;
  Always put first things first."

She went to the summer camp with the rest,
  But everything seemed to conspire
To distract her still, as they sat in a ring
  And cooked by an altar fire.

They sang, "Green grow the rushes, oh,"
  But she paused at the refrain
As she thought of the cymbals at her door
  And days in the April rain.

He ran on an orienteering course
  And steered by the lonely pole;
But magnetic attraction came into his mind
  And he almost lost control.

The wind fanned the camp-fire into flames;
  The moon sailed into view;
They sang, "One is one and all alone";
  He thought, "Evermore be true."

At seventeen, she was a Ranger Guide;
  He was a Venture Scout;
There in the empty fairground
  Stood the swings and roundabout.

They followed their independent paths;
  Each won the Gold Award.
He went to the Palace, unknown to her;
  She heard the guests applaud.

He shook hands with the duke - and then he saw,
  To his unconfined surprise,
That among the close-knit ranks of Guides
  Was a girl with hazel eyes.

They walked on the Palace's elegant lawns,
  Discreetly, hand in hand,
And toyed with cucumber sandwiches
  To the tunes of a different band.

"Will you walk with me now?" he quietly said,
  Now that our prizes are won,
For I think we should tie the knot of knots
  That will never be undone."

"I will," she said, as she drew him close,
  "For you see, I did decide
If you ever came scouting for a wife
  That love should be our guide."

LOVE
See also MARRIAGE

She was a library assistant,
    One hesitant foot on the rung;
He was ascending the ladder -
    His praises were frequently sung.

She worked at the Reference counter
    In a humble, repetitive way;
He came down from Classification
    And Cataloguing, once every day.

She cautiously watched from a distance,
    As he carefully sorted and filed;
Then she dropped all the books she was shelving,
    And he stopped, and he looked, and he smiled.

She worked on the magazine counter,
    And she dreamed of becoming his wife,
And she handed out "Woman" and "Mother"
    Instead of back numbers of "Life".

At last came the hoped-for promotion;
    She numbered the books by his side,
And the merest of glances he gave her
    Made her feel (shall we say) dewy-eyed.

They met in the mobile presses
    And he gave her a passionate kiss;
She said, "Is this the Library of Congress?"
    He said, "No, but it's certainly Bliss."

She frowned: "Six-four-one's not my number;
    In the kitchen, I get in a fix."
He said, "Don't worry, my darling;
    I prefer ... six-one-two... point six."

And so they were happily married,
    Not later, or sometime, but soon;
Their romance was a suitable fiction
    From the pages of Mills and Boon,

For our lives are in need of some poetry
    Before we're discarded or gone;
Some loves and some smiles and some laughter;
    In short, some eight-twenty-one.

                         *

SHAKESPEARE LIMERICKS

In Arden, the world is a stage.
Rosalind's dressed as a page,
        A clown buys a ring
        For an ill-favoured thing,
And Jacques is feeling his age.

                         *

A book full of Prospero's tricks,
Some courtiers caught in a fix,
        An aerial fairy,
        A monster (quite scary),
And love at first sight: what a mix!

Said Hamlet: "Poor father! His brother,
My uncle, has married my mother;
    Ophelia's a curse,
    Polonius is worse -
A duel? We'll kill one another."

         *

"He dies on the Ides," say the seers;
Antony borrows some ears;
    A ghost in the air
    Makes Brutus despair;
Of course, it'll all end in spears.

         *

Three witches, a cauldron a-bubble.
A wife who is nothing but trouble,
    A murderous plot
    And a damnable spot,
And trees that approach at the double.

         *

A queen with a changeable smile,
A barge that is burnished in style,
    Disaster aboard,
    An asp and a sword:
The answer is death on the Nile.

         *

Juliet burns like a flame
For Romeo - what's in a name?
   Well, there is a vendetta
   And an overdue letter,
But fate - or the stars - get the blame.

*

Leontes suspects an affair;
A keeper's snapped up by a bear:
   The years hurry round,
   And Perdita's found,
And a statue makes everyone stare.

*

ENGLISH HAIKU

Recent research has shown that the haiku was discovered
in this country much earlier than was previously thought.

J.M.

Pensive mood, be gone:
Come, Sabrina, and restore
My native wood-notes.

A.P.

Fortunate monarchs,
Penned in heroic measure,
Not this tiny verse.

W.W.

Sheep on fell and crag,
Wondrous sight like fleecy clouds:
I count seventeen.

H.W.L.

Hiawatha's lost,
Done to death by the Trochees:
Weep, Minnehaha.

W.B.Y.

Put pen to paper,
An emerald mist descends:
I can see fairies.

T.S.E.

Your shadow rises
In the morning to meet you:
Then it disappears.

D.T.

The town sleeps: I wake
To celebrate the green spring ...
Just three lines, you said?

J.B.

Too old for tennis,
I sublimate my desires
In wicked verses.

P.A.

My baby's six foot,
His rugby kit that mucky!
More work than nappies.

A.M.

Poets Laureate
When short of inspiration
Go through the motions.

THE COMPUTER'S FAREWELL TO ITS MASTER

Tell me master must you go?
Kindly answer yes or no
Do not interrupt my flow
Tell me what I need to know

I can handle long division
Treat quadratics with derision
But from you I need precision
I can't cope with indecision

Must you leave your homely nest?
Are your actions for the best?
Here's a really simple test
Logic sets the mind at rest

If you're leaving here today
This was also true last May
True a hundred years away
You are programmed not to stay

Therefore you're no longer free
Things are what they had to be
You are you and I am me
You're the lock and I'm the key

You will reach your destination
Terminal or railway station
Ruled by binary notation
Let me end with some quotation

Drawn from Emerson and Thoreau
Here today and gone tomorrow
Never lend what you can borrow
Parting is the sweetest sorrow

Master

THE WORLD'S SHORTEST POEMS

Hai

Seventeen syllables
Is far too many.
I prefer sixteen.

Lim

Dear
Lear.
Dead.
Shed
A tear.

Son

Earth hath not anything to show more fair:
If that's the case, I may as well stop there.

Net
(The world's shortest love poem)

Shall I compare thee to a summer's day?
Poor fool, I love another: hence, away!

Quest

They followed their instructions to the letter:
Endured the desert, found the spring, felt better.

Epic

Sing, Muse, of Trojan war and Odyssey,
Of Dido and Aeneas, birth of Rome,
Of Beowulf, Valhalla, and the Ring,
Thus ending with the Twilight of the Gods.

LINES OF THOUGHT

Let me explain
  (I feel I ought)
Convergent and
  Divergent thought.

Convergent thought
  Is what we know.
Pure logic: charts
  Define the flow.

A brick is used
  To build a wall:
It has no other
  Use at all.

Convergent thinkers
  Do not swerve:
They think in lines
  And never curve.

Some want to rule
  The world we're in,
And shape a cube
  That cannot spin.

Divergence is
  The way things seem;
Divergent thinkers
  Often dream.

Their conversation
  Breezes past,
Each topic quite
  Unlike the last.

A brick, if dropped,
  May break the ice,
Or split in half
  Can serve as dice.

A smaller part,
  If ground to dust,
Would fill an hour-glass
  You can trust.

Re-used, some make
  The new seem old,
Or wrapped in foil
  Resemble gold.

Such thoughts, by their
  Poetic flight,
Can spin the world,
  Create the light;

Without them, night
  Would shortly fall,
And life would not
  Be life at all.

MUSICAL THEMES

Ralph Vaughan Williams (1872-1958)
The "Tallis Fantasia" was first performed in Gloucester Cathedral, the "cool, reflective place". The "strident anthem" is in "Sancta Civitas". R.V.W collected "strands of folk-song". "The troubled hill" is Wenlock Edge in the title-poem of the A.E. Housman song-cycle.
"The breakers roll" in "A Sea Symphony"; "the clock-tower's chime" is heard in "A London Symphony", the "sounds of war" in the Sixth, and the "muffled drums and dead bells" in "Sinfonia Antartica".
"The celestial city" is in the opera "A Pilgrim's Progress".

Gustav Holst (1874-1934)
Verse 4 refers to "A Choral Symphony": a setting of poems by Keats, including "Ode on a Grecian Urn" and "Fancy's Song". Holst was a trombone-player, not a "Mystic Trumpeter", and "The Perfect Fool" is an opera. He also collected "tunes we sang". "Ostinato" and "Dargason" are movements from the "St. Paul's Suite". In verse 6, "The Hymn of Jesus" includes settings of the plain-song hymns "Pangue lingua" and "Vexilla regis", partly in dance-rhythm. All the movements of the "Planets" suite are represented or implied.

Edward Elgar (1857-1934)
This imitates the pattern of "The Enigma Variations".
C.A.E.- his wife Caroline Alice Elgar: A.J.J.- August Jaeger ("Nimrod"): D.P. - Dora Penny ("Dorabella"): H.J.W. - Henry Wood, founder of the Proms: "the march" - "Pomp and Circumstance No. 1" was the only double *orchestral* encore: G.B.S. was also a music critic: H.R. - Hans Richter: "The Dream of Gerontius" was under-rehearsed for its first performance: Y.M. - Yehudi Menuhin performed the Violin Concerto, which is prefaced by words "Aqui esta encerrada el alma de ..." (Here lies hidden the soul of ...): K.F. - Kathleen Ferrier sang the Angel in "The Dream": "always ...always ... ": refers to her moving performance of Mahler - "Das Lied von der Erde", ending "ewig ... ewig ..." (forever ... forever ...). T.E.L. - T.E. Lawrence.
"The Music-Makers" - setting of poem by Arthur O'Shaughnessy: "I went to sleep ... " - opening of Part II of "The Dream": "My life..." - words from John Ruskin's "Sesame and Lilies", written by Elgar on the completed score of "The Dream of Gerontius".

Carl Nielsen (1865-1931)

The "shoemaker's son" was Hans Christian Andersen. "The sculptress" was Anne Marie Brodersen. "Springtime on Fyn" is a choral work. He grew up on the island of Fyn (Funen). "The wordless voices" occur in the slow movement of the Third Symphony (Sinfonia espansiva). The "thunder" is the timpani in the finale of the Fourth Symphony ("The Inextinguishable"), and the "side-drummer" tries - and fails - to halt the flow of the Fifth. "The prince's ship" sails in "The Little Mermaid". "The Steadfast Tin Soldier" (Andersen): Nielsen refused to give in to heart trouble. "His monument", by his wife, is in Copenhagen. "Thou Danish man" is a much-loved folk-song setting.

Jean Sibelius (1865-1957)

Kalevala was the ancient name for Finland, and the title of the epic poem which re-told their legends. Vainamoinen was a national hero. Lemminkainen was his companion. Pohjola was the cold country of the north (Lapland); "Pohjola's daughter" is a symphonic poem. Karelia lies in eastern Finland, and gave its name to an orchestral suite, while "Finlandia" is a patriotic symphonic poem. Tuonela is the land of the dead: "The Swan of Tuonela " is one of four "Legends for Orchestra" (the "Lemminkainen" Suite). Tapiola is the sombre domain of Tapio, the god of the northern forests, and the name for a symphonic poem. Sibelius tended to break up complete themes into fragments of melody, or make fragments into themes.

"Gaspard de la Nuit"

Piano suite in three movements by Ravel: "Ondine", "Le Gibet", "Scarbo" (order reversed in the poem): based on fables by 19th. century writer Aloysius Bertrand.

"Under Water"

"Carillon ... " : Debussy Preludes Book I: "La cathédrale engloutie" (The submerged cathedral), based on Breton legend of the city of Ys. "Orchestral rhythms" and "hymn of waves and air" are allusions to Debussy's orchestral suite "La Mer".

These last two poems employ "scattered rhyme": pairs of rhymes spread throughout the poems.

GLOUCESTER: A RELIABLE HISTORY

c.49   Romans build legionary fort at Kingsholm (now home of Gloucester R.F.C.).

c.65   New fortress on site of present city centre.

c.96   Colonia (home for retired veterans) founded.

The Roman and mediaeval East Gate can be seen outside Boots. The emperor Caligula was given little boots by soldiers when a child: hence the nickname.

577   Battle of Dyrham gave Saxons control of three cities.

679   Foundation of St. Peter's monastery by King Osric.

909   The city re-fortified by Queen Aethelflaeda.

1066   William of Normandy held Great Council in the city.

1085   Order for Domesday Book signed by William in city.

1089   Serlo, Bishop of Bayeux, begins building of new abbey of St. Peter: growth of mediaeval monastery begins.

1216   Henry III (aged nine) crowned in abbey.

1327   Body of Edward II received by abbey.

1455   100, Westgate Street occupied by Richard Whittington, possibly a nephew of Dick Whittington.

c.1500   Two inns built by abbey for pilgrims visiting tomb of Edward II. There is no evidence of underground passages.

1535   Henry VIII and Anne Boleyn visit city; go hunting at Painswick.

1540   Jan. 2nd. St. Peter's Abbey surrendered by Prior to Royal
        Commissioners: Abbey becomes Cathedral of new diocese
        of Gloucester: monastic buildings preserved.

1555   Feb. 9th. John Hooper, second Bishop of Gloucester, burnt at
        stake for maintaining Protestant beliefs. Memorial built 1862.

1635   June 8th.- 9th. Rev. Dr. Nathaniel Brent (Doctor of Law), visits
        city to inspect churches, as ordered by Archbishop Laud.
        Probable origin of "Doctor Foster" rhymes.

1643   10th. Aug.- 5th. Sept. City on side of Parliament in Civil War.
        Besieged by Royalist army. Resistance led by Edward Massey.
        "Humpty Dumpty" thought to refer to collapse of siege engine
        propped against city walls. "The pig ... " Humorous poem by
        H.Y.J.Taylor: a squealing pig suggests that food is plentiful.

1661   Charles II orders destruction of city walls.

c.1719 First Music Meeting held (later Three Choirs Festival).

1751   High Cross taken down.

1787   Demolition of ruined castle keep begins.

1812   New Docks basin completed.

1827   Gloucester-Sharpness Canal completed.

1962   Jellicoe Plan proposes Via Sacra close to line of city walls.

1971   "The Onedin Line" begins: some scenes filmed in Docks.

1971   Three local archaeologists (including the illustrator of this
        book) examine timber frame of Southern's Stores before
        demolition: they are influential in forming Gloucester Civic
        Trust for preservation of city's historic buildings.